Cooking for Mum

by Swapna Haddow
Illustrated by Emma Trithart

OXFORD
UNIVERSITY PRESS

adult

Nani was looking after Yash and Meena while Mum was at work. They were going to cook some stuffed rotis for Mum.

Yash, Meena and Nani went to the supermarket to get some roti flour. They searched <u>among</u> the shelves but, by the time they found the flour, the children were tired.

"We've been shopping <u>forever</u>," Yash moaned. "My feet ache."

"Right, let's go home," said Nani.

Yash is complaining that they have been shopping for a long time. It feels like <u>forever</u> to him. Are there any activities that you do that seem to take <u>forever</u>?

child

They went to Tom's flat.
"Help, Tom!" said Yash. "We are out of butter."

"We have got lots," Tom said.
He handed Meena a packet of butter.

adult

They were finally ready to cook. The children washed their hands and rolled up their sleeves.

Meena poured the flour into a bowl.

Yash added some oil and water.

"Mix them together until you have a ball of dough," Nani said. "You will need powerful muscles for this job!"

Why do you think the children need powerful muscles to mix the dough? Do you think it will be an easy job or a hard job?

The mixture fell.
"We will mop it up," Meena said.

adult

The children quickly cleaned up the mess. Then they worked together to make a new batch of dough.

"I'm pleased to see you've stopped fighting and are being friendly," said Nani.

Meena and Yash shared the rolling pin, taking it in turns to flatten the rotis into circles.

Nani began frying the rotis while the children kept a safe distance from the hot butter.

 Instead of fighting, Yash and Meena are being friendly. What have they done to show they are now being friendly to each other?

child

"They *are* good," said Mum. "You can sell them!"

"Good plan," agreed Meena.

Yash and Meena were keen to get cooking.

child

adult

The next day …

There was a show at the school. Yash and Meena asked if they could sell their rotis to the <u>audience</u>.

During the break, Meena called out: "Delicious rotis!"

Everyone loved the rotis. Yash and Meena made lots of money for the school. All the <u>effort</u> had been worth it.

Yash and Meena sold their rotis to the audience at the school show. Have you ever been part of an <u>audience</u>? What were you watching?

"Look!" Yash said. "It's Tom."
"You can have this as a gift," Meena said.

Thank you.

Yash and Meena put a lot of effort into making the rotis. Does that mean they worked hard or not very hard? Why was all the effort they put in worth it?

Making rotis!

Can you explain how to make a roti?